BUILT FOR SUCCESS

THE STORY OF

Microsoft

First published in the UK in 2011 by
Franklin Watts
338 Euston Road
London NW1 3BH

Franklin Watts Australia
Level 17/207 Kent Street
Sydney, NSW 2000

First published by Creative Education,
an imprint of The Creative Company.
Copyright © 2009 Creative Education.
A CIP catalogue record for this book is available from the
British Library.

ISBN: 978 1 4451 0594 9
Dewey number: 338.7'610053

Printed in China

Franklin Watts is a division of
Hachette Children's Books,
an Hachette UK company.
www.hachette.co.uk

DESIGN AND PRODUCTION BY **ZENO DESIGN**

PHOTOGRAPHS BY Alamy (Artpartner-images.com, Frank
Chmura, Dave Jepson, Ian Shaw, Vario Images GmbH & Co.
KG), Corbis (NATION BILL, Bettmann, Kevin P. Casey, Najlah
Feanny, Wolfgang Kaehler, Dan Lamont, Matthew Mcvay,
Jim Sugar, TWPhoto, Doug Wilson, Naashon Zalk), Getty
Images (China Photos, Sam Forencich/NBA, Joe McNally,
Diana Walker/Liaison, Ron Wurzer)

BUILT FOR SUCCESS

THE STORY OF

Microsoft

W
FRANKLIN WATTS
LONDON • SYDNEY

NELL MUSOLF

Former Microsoft chief software architect Ray Ozzie (2006–2010) [see page 40].

spresso machines in every office building. Private offices where workers are encouraged merely to 'sit and think' free of distractions. The faint hum of computers filling the air. Such is everyday life in Redmond, Washington, USA, at the headquarters of Microsoft Corporation, a giant in the world of computing software. Since it was founded in 1975, Microsoft has become one of the most famous and successful companies in the world. Through its innovative, user-friendly software, Microsoft was one of the pioneers responsible for bringing the personal computer into the lives of millions of people. The company's impact has been such that the name 'Microsoft' is now virtually synonymous with computer software – and it all began three decades ago with two young men who were captivated by computers.

The early days

Although computers were being built and used as early as the 1930s, they didn't enter the modern age until the 1960s. The first personal computers of the early 1960s did not have much in common with personal computers of today. Those early machines were bulky, expensive and used primarily by businesses, hospitals and large universities that could afford them.

Since they did not have their own computers, it was common practice for small schools to hire computer time from larger schools or universities. In 1967, at Lakeside School, a private secondary school in the Seattle, Washington area, the Lakeside Mothers Club held a fund-raiser to hire computer time for the students. After raising £1,870 ($3,000) the club members thought they would be able to purchase ample computer time for the entire student body. But they hadn't counted on the interest of two Year 8 students called Kent Evans and Bill Gates. Fascinated by computers ever since a maths teacher had taken them to see the school's ASR-33 Teletype, a machine used to send typed messages from one point to another electronically, Evans and Gates spent all the time they could on the computer the

Although fairly simplistic, the Teletype electronic typewriter fascinated Kent Evans and Bill Gates

Lakeside Mothers Club had leased for them. The £1,870 ($3,000) worth of computer time was quickly consumed.

Evans and Gates soon formed the Lakeside Programmers Club, a group devoted to writing computer programs. They were joined by Paul Allen and Rick Weiland, two secondary school students who were also intrigued by computers. The Lakeside Programmers Club landed several jobs for the young **entrepreneurs** which included developing a payroll system for a local business and computerising their own school's class schedules.

One day, while working at the computer, Gates remarked to Allen, "Don't you think that someday everybody will have one of these things? And if they did, couldn't you deliver magazines and newspapers and stuff through them?" Gates' comment was a remarkably accurate prediction of the future of the personal computer.

Throughout their years at Lakeside School, Allen and Gates spent as much time as they could working on computers, becoming good friends in the process. After the tragic death of Kent Evans in a mountain climbing accident, their friendship grew stronger. It was the beginning of a lifelong partnership that would eventually become one of the biggest successes in the history of American business.

In 1969, a general-purpose **computer chip** was invented by Ted Hoff, a researcher at the Intel Corporation. With the invention, which enabled computers to be built more quickly and cheaply, personal computers took a major step forwards in becoming more accessible to the average consumer.

Six years later, the January 1975 issue of *Popular Electronics* magazine featured the Altair 8800, calling it the world's 'first mini-computer'. In fact, the Altair was more of an electronic kit than a computer. For £250 ($397) the kit could be purchased through the post and assembled at home. When completed, the Altair was a metal box with flashing lights and switches, and there wasn't much to do with it other than play noughts and crosses. But that didn't matter

Bill Gates (left) and Paul Allen (right), shown here in 1983, were obsessed with computers in secondary school to computer enthusiasts. In one afternoon, MITS (Micro Instrumentation and Telemetry Systems), the company that made the Altair, took 400 orders for the computer. In three weeks, MITS earned £156,000 ($250,000).

Allen spotted the issue of *Popular Electronics* one day on his way to visit Gates at Harvard University, where Gates was then a student. At the time, Allen was working for Honeywell, an electronics company. From their years of study and experimentation Allen and Gates were well acquainted with the two principle parts of a computer: the **hardware** and software. Hardware refers to the physical parts, or the mechanisms, of the computer. Software includes the programs that run the computer, or tell the hardware what to do. After reading the article on the Altair 8800, the two friends agreed that the growing world of personal computers was going to need a great deal of software.

Allen and Gates contacted MITS owner Ed Roberts in 1975. They told him that they would create an easy-to-use computer language based on a 1960s general-purpose programming language called BASIC (Beginner's All-purpose Symbolic Instruction Code), and that their program would enable the Altair 8800 to interpret the BASIC language program. What Allen and Gates told Roberts wasn't completely true; they hadn't actually written their version of BASIC yet but they were confident that they could. Roberts agreed to try their program. In less than five weeks, working around the clock, Allen and Gates finished their version of BASIC. It became known as Altair BASIC.

When the Altair BASIC program was completed, Allen flew to Albuquerque, New Mexico, where MITS was located. All of the time and work that Allen and Gates had put into Altair BASIC paid off. Altair BASIC was efficient and easy to use, giving users increased memory and the familiarity of the BASIC computer language. After seeing how well Altair BASIC worked, MITS offered Allen a job, and in March 1975, he left his position at Honeywell and moved to Albuquerque. Gates remained at Harvard but kept in close contact with Allen. With the success of Altair BASIC, Allen and Gates planned to continue their partnership in the burgeoning world of computer software.

The DEC PDP-8 Microcomputer

Digital Equipment Corporation introduced the PDP family of minicomputers in the 1960s. As classmates, Bill Gates and Paul Allen convinced a local computer company to give them free access to its PDP in exchange for finding flaws in the system.

The Altair 8800 offered Bill Gates and Paul Allen a chance to devise their own computer language

Chinese police examining pirated software

A LETTER TO ENTHUSIASTS

When Paul Allen and Bill Gates sold their version of BASIC to MITS in 1975, they signed a licensing agreement which stated that they would make money from the sale of their software if it was sold as part of the Altair or if it was sold separately. Gates in particular was concerned about the possibility of software copying by computer enthusiasts, a practice known as 'pirating'. In 'An Open Letter to Hobbyists [Enthusiasts]', published in *Computer Notes* magazine in 1976, Gates argued that copying software was tantamount to stealing it and that software developers needed the protection of copyright laws similar to the laws that protected songwriters. The letter didn't have a huge effect on computer users and no copyright laws were created at that time. Computer users still seemed to prefer 'borrowing' software from each other instead of buying their own copies, a problem Microsoft eventually addressed by increasing security measures on all of its software.

The rise of Microsoft

After completing his second year at university, Gates went to Albuquerque for the summer of 1975. It was then that he and Allen decided to start their own software company. They originally called their company "Micro-Soft" but a few months later dropped the hyphen, and the company became known as Microsoft. Gates returned to Harvard that autumn but left in 1977 before graduating to devote himself full-time to Microsoft.

Allen and Gates weren't the only people seeking new ways to improve personal computers. In 1976, Steve Jobs and Steve Wozniak, two young computer enthusiasts from Palo Alto, California, unveiled the **prototype** for the Apple I computer. A local computer dealer saw the Apple I and ordered 100 pre-assembled units. Over the next 10 months around 200 Apple I units were sold.

One year later, Jobs and Wozniak introduced the Apple II personal computer. The Apple II was sold already assembled, with 4 kilobytes (kb) of **RAM**, or memory. It was simple to operate and featured colour **graphics**, something no other personal computer had at that time. But, like all computers, the Apple II needed software. Jobs and Wozniak wanted to include software such as games and word-processing

Steve Jobs's development of Apple Computer in the late 1970s created software opportunities for Microsoft programs free of charge with the purchase of their computer. After learning of Jobs and Wozniak's plans, Microsoft sold the Apple Computer company a software programme called Applesoft BASIC, a programming language that allowed Apple II users to perform more technical **applications** than Apple I's had been able to do. Apple sold more than one million computers in the late 1970s, each with a copy of Applesoft BASIC installed.

In 1978, Allen and Gates decided to move Microsoft from Albuquerque to the Pacific Northwest area of the USA, where they'd both grown up. The next year Microsoft – then made up of Gates, Allen and nine other staff members – moved its headquarters to Bellevue, Washington.

In 1980, Steve Ballmer joined Microsoft as first assistant to president Bill Gates. Before moving to Microsoft, Ballmer had worked at Proctor and Gamble, a consumer products company, as a deputy project manager. A friend of Gates from their days at Harvard, Ballmer took over many of the administrative duties Gates had been handling.

Also in 1980, Allen and Gates began wearing business suits and ties instead of their usual jeans and casual shirts to discuss a possible contract with the International Business Machines (IBM) Company. IBM needed software to provide language and operating systems, or software that enabled the operation of various other programs, for its first personal computers. After securing the contract Microsoft was suddenly the supplier of vital software to a giant in the computer industry. To meet IBM's needs, Gates and Allen created MS-DOS (Microsoft Disk Operating System) from a language called Q-DOS which they had purchased from the Seattle Computer Products company. In a move considered questionable by some, Microsoft didn't tell Seattle Computer Products about its impending deal with IBM. Instead it simply said it had a customer that needed a program similar to Q-DOS. Microsoft then negotiated with IBM to retain separate **marketing** rights for the operating system. Q-DOS became PC-DOS for IBM, while MS-DOS was Microsoft's version.

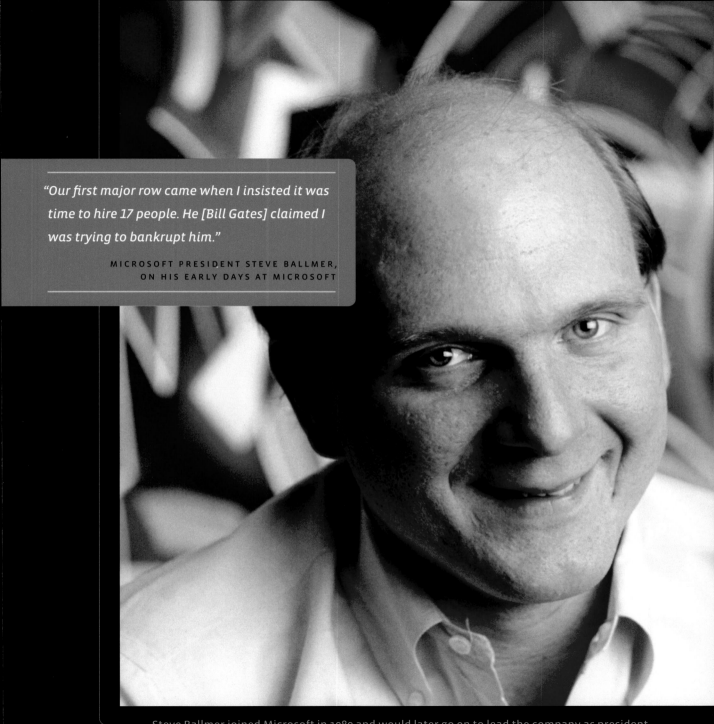

> "Our first major row came when I insisted it was time to hire 17 people. He [Bill Gates] claimed I was trying to bankrupt him."
>
> MICROSOFT PRESIDENT STEVE BALLMER, ON HIS EARLY DAYS AT MICROSOFT

Steve Ballmer joined Microsoft in 1980 and would later go on to lead the company as president

Hundreds of thousands of computers were sold in the early 1980s and a copy of MS-DOS was sold along with almost every one. Microsoft had become the crucial connection between the hardware and software needed to operate computers. The huge sales of MS-DOS fuelled Microsoft's financial growth, increasing the company's annual revenue from £10 million ($16 million) in 1981 to £15.3 million ($24.5 million) in 1982.

February 1983 marked a big change at Microsoft. After learning that he had Hodgkin's disease, a type of cancer, Paul Allen resigned from his position as executive vice president of Microsoft. After successful medical treatment Allen remained on the board of directors at Microsoft but stepped down permanently from daily operations, choosing instead to devote his time to other interests beyond computers, such as sailing and various **philanthropic** endeavours.

Another important event unfolded in 1983. When Steve Jobs told Microsoft about Apple's newest technology, the Macintosh computer, or the 'Mac', Microsoft signed a contract with Apple to develop software programmes that could run on the Macintosh. Gates asked his researchers to develop a **GUI**, or **graphical user interface**, which could be used on IBM-compatible machines as well. In that way Microsoft stood to make a profit by providing software systems for both Apple and IBM computers.

The Macintosh was simple to use and popular with consumers, but in 1983, IBM was still the largest and most important company in the computer hardware industry. Since IBM had chosen to use Microsoft's software, other hardware companies such as Tandy and Commodore also chose to use Microsoft. To keep up with their expanding list of clients, Microsoft soon hired more programmers, managers and office support staff, increasing Microsoft's payroll to 476 employees in 1983 as annual sales passed £31 million ($50 million). "Bill [Gates] has done a great job of cloning himself as the company has grown. Now there are all these aggressive "Little Bills"... and they keep coming at you and coming at you," Steve Jobs said.

"To be 30 years old and have that kind of shock – to face your own mortality – makes you feel like you should do some of the things that you haven't done."

PAUL ALLEN, MICROSOFT EXECUTIVE

Paul Allen made various investments after 1983; in 2003, he financed the history-making private spacecraft *SpaceShipOne*

COMPUTER IN A CHIP

When Intel researcher Ted Hoff invented the first **silicon** computer chip in 1969, it was a major step towards putting computers into homes as well as offices. Computer chips are tiny pieces of material, typically silicon, that contain an electronic circuit. The two major types of computer chips are microprocessors which carry out the instructions of a computer program, and memory chips which hold programs and information. Microprocessor chips are used in computers, video games, digital watches, microwave ovens and some telephones. Memory chips are divided into two categories: ones with read-only memory (ROM), and ones with random-access memory (RAM). ROM chips hold on to their memory even when the computer is switched off. RAM chips hold their memory only as long as the computer has power. Without computer chips, personal computers might never have been invented, and firms such as Microsoft might not exist.

Windows to the world

Late in 1983, Microsoft introduced its most advanced word-processing program to date, Microsoft Word, and also announced the creation of the program Windows, which would be released in 1985. Windows was a true innovation in computers as it allowed users to open more than one document at the same time.

Microsoft's computer **mouse**, similar to the Mac's mouse, was another new item. The mouse let people simply point at and click on an on-screen command instead of typing in lines of commands, thus reducing keystrokes and work time.

But in spite of its innovative features Windows received negative reviews from users. Microsoft had hurried its programmers to complete Windows and get it on the market as quickly as possible. As a result, Windows had significant limitations – for example, open documents, or 'windows', could not overlap one another on the screen – and used up a great deal of computer memory, causing computers to freeze, or 'crash'. Microsoft programmers were compelled to go back into Windows and repair the problems.

In addition to being blamed for rushing a product into shops before it was ready, Microsoft also found itself accused of indulging in a marketing tactic known in the computer world as 'vapourware'. Vapourware refers to a ploy by which a company

With the introduction of Windows Bill Gates helped change computer history by making multi-tasking simple

MICROSOFT

PAGE 24

BUILT FOR SUCCESS

announces a product well before it is ready to be sold to consumers. By practising vapourware, Microsoft could discourage potential customers from buying a competitor's product before Microsoft's product was available, such as when Microsoft announced the impending arrival of the first Windows well before the product was complete. Microsoft was also occasionally charged with buying out their competitors' products from shops so that customers had no choice but to purchase a Microsoft product, an allegation that Microsoft denied.

In summer 1985 construction began on new corporate headquarters – soon to become known as Microsoft Place – in Redmond, Washington. The casual, relaxed atmosphere at Microsoft Place and the young age of most of the employees led many people to compare it to a university campus. Set in a wooded area, some of the buildings were designed in an 'X' shape to receive the maximum amount of sunlight. Consisting of 41 buildings and covering 109 hectares (270 acres) the complex also had footpaths and a playing field for programmers and office staff to use when they needed a break. A large pond in the middle of the grounds was dubbed "Lake Bill" in honour of the company's president.

Microsoft celebrated its 10th year in business in 1985. Over that decade, Microsoft had grown into a major corporation employing 900 people and enjoying annual sales of £87 million ($140 million). By 1986, Microsoft had increased its employee ranks to 1,153 and its **stock** went public, meaning people outside the company were allowed to became part-owners. The first day the stock went on the market Microsoft earned £38 million ($61 million). Within one year, 31-year-old Bill Gates would be a billionaire.

Windows 2.0 was launched in 1987, an event that marked the beginning of a legal battle with Apple Computer. The previously friendly relationship Microsoft and Apple had enjoyed changed when, in 1988, Apple brought a lawsuit against Microsoft, claiming that the idea for Windows had been taken from Apple's designs. Microsoft countered that both Windows and Mac systems used

The vast Microsoft Place, which opened in 1986, today accommodates more than 30,000 Microsoft employees different features taken from the same source: Xerox's Alto computer. Xerox didn't sell its computer system, so the features it used could be integrated by any company. Apple then brought a second lawsuit against Microsoft which claimed that Microsoft had illegally copied aspects – such as its rectangular boxes containing commands – of Macintosh's operating system. Microsoft would ultimately win both cases in the US federal court in 1992.

Microsoft's relationship with IBM was also troubled in 1988. Microsoft designed a software package called OS/2 for IBM at the same time Windows 2.0 was created, causing IBM to worry that Windows 2.0 would take customers away from OS/2. IBM's fears were realised when Windows 2.0 outsold IBM's OS/2 by a wide margin, not because OS/2 wasn't technically sound but because, many people believed, of Microsoft's effective marketing for Windows 2.0.

Windows 3.0 was completed and released in 1990 with the largest marketing campaign in Microsoft's history. It was a hit with computer users from the moment it came on the market, due primarily to a major redesign that included larger memory support as well as a more colourful user interface. Windows 3.0 was so profitable that in 1990 Microsoft became the first computer software company ever to top £625 million ($1 billion) in sales. "Windows, Windows, Windows!" Steve Ballmer chanted at company meetings as the software programme sold 100,000 copies during its first two weeks on the market. Microsoft would continue cheering as it became – and remained – the world's undisputed leader in software throughout the 1990s.

The success of Windows 3.0 only irritated IBM further and IBM renewed its accusations that Microsoft intentionally had put less effort into the programmes it designed for IBM so that Windows 3.0 would win a larger share of the market. In addition, Windows 3.0 wasn't compatible with OS/2, so people who chose to use Windows 3.0 would not be able to work on an IBM computer. More lawsuits were levelled against Microsoft. It wouldn't be the last time the company would be accused of not dealing fairly with competitors.

IBM, the world's largest computer company, and Microsoft have had an up-and-down relationship

As Microsoft became phenomenally successful, Bill Gates and his wife, Melinda, became philanthropists and created the Bill and Melinda Gates Foundation. While the Foundation has both local and global goals, it strives primarily to reduce poverty, improve healthcare and help educate people everywhere. It believes that through science and technology people's lives can be improved. Since it was founded in 1994, it has created grant commitments, or promises of money, of £15.23 billion ($24.45 billion). In 2010, total grant payments reached £1.6 billion ($2.6 billion). By applying scientific and technological innovations – such as supplying vaccines to help prevent childhood diseases – the Foundation helps the world's neediest people. As the Gateses state on the foundation's website, "We... believe that from those to whom much is given, much is expected. We benefited from great schools, great healthcare and a vibrant economic system. That is why we feel a tremendous responsibility to give back to society."

The age of the Internet

The 1990s ushered in another period of growth at Microsoft. In 1991, Microsoft introduced the Microsoft Ballpoint Mouse, a mouse designed to work with **laptop computers**. The Microsoft Ballpoint Mouse clamped onto the side of the computer and used no desk space, allowing users to easily navigate a computer screen any time, anywhere.

Two years later, Microsoft Encarta, a multimedia encyclopaedia which contained all the information of a traditional set of encyclopaedias on one **CD-ROM**, was unveiled. Another 1993 innovation was the Mouse 2.0, a new mouse designed for comfortable use by both left-handed and right-handed users. The year ended with *Fortune* magazine calling Microsoft the 'Most Innovative Company Working in the United States'.

By 1995, as Microsoft celebrated its 20th anniversary, the company had grown to more than 16,350 employees. In August of that year, Windows 95 was released to great fanfare. With its easy installation and ability to be customised to the individual user, Windows 95 promised to outperform all previous versions of Windows. Microsoft promoted its latest Windows with parties, television advertisements and high-profile media events; the famous Empire State Building in New York City, for example,

Whether on T-shirts or the Empire State Building, Windows 95 was a big news story in August 1995

was illuminated in the red, green, blue and yellow colours of the Windows logo. The advertising strategy worked; after just four days on the market more than one million copies of Windows 95 had been sold in North America. More than seven million copies were sold worldwide by October.

Microsoft leapt into the Internet age by rolling out the Microsoft Network (MSN), a full-service Internet provider, in 1995. Three months after its launch the network had more than 500,000 members. Later that same year, Microsoft introduced a new version of MSN called Microsoft Internet Explorer, which was a more advanced Internet **browser**. Before 1995 ended, Microsoft – along with US television network NBC – had created a new 24-hour news channel called MSNBC and a corresponding online news service.

A reunion occurred between Microsoft and Apple in 1997. In spite of the difficulties the two companies had encountered in the past, they came to the realisation that they could make better products working together than they could working apart. Under the new arrangement Microsoft would produce future versions of Microsoft Office, Internet Explorer and other tools for the Macintosh, and the two companies would share a wide **patent** and **cross-licencing** agreement. Microsoft would also invest £93 million ($150 million) in Apple, while Apple would make Microsoft's Internet Explorer the **default** browser link to the Internet on its new computers.

In 1998, a change occurred in the corporate structure at Microsoft when Steve Ballmer was appointed president. Gates, the former president, remained chairman and chief executive officer (CEO) of Microsoft. Microsoft also made news in 1998 when its Internet Explorer sparked one of the biggest lawsuits in the history of American business.

The lawsuit came about when the US Department of Justice alleged that Microsoft had broken **anti-trust laws**. When Microsoft created its Windows 98 operating system, the Microsoft Internet Explorer browser was included automatically with any computer that ran on the Windows operating system.

Network connections. Microsoft leapt into the world of the Internet in the mid-1990s with Internet Explorer

The US Department of Justice believed that, by including Microsoft Internet Explorer with its software packages, Microsoft was trying to force other browser companies out of the market. It was difficult for smaller companies such as Netscape and the fledgling America Online (AOL) to compete in the Internet browser market because Microsoft's product was sold with so many computers. The US Department of Justice also claimed that Microsoft was close to having a **monopoly** and had used its power to force Internet service providers into exclusive deals using Microsoft Internet Explorer.

In response to these charges Microsoft asserted that it was largely responsible for the Internet revolution of the 1990s, a revolution that had been highly beneficial for the US economy. In order to reduce Microsoft's enormous clout in the software world, the government recommended that it include other browsers such as Netscape and AOL, along with Internet Explorer, in its software packages. Not surprisingly, this suggestion was unpopular amongst Microsoft executives. "It would be like asking Coca-Cola to ship three Pepsis with every six-pack," one remarked after hearing the government's idea.

Microsoft defended itself by claiming that it had planned to include Internet Explorer with its software packages before Netscape and other companies were even founded. Company officials said that computer manufacturers included Internet Explorer on their systems because it was a good browser program, not because Microsoft forced them to do so. "Our success is based on only one thing: good products," said Gates. "It's not very complicated. We're not powerful enough to cause products that are not excellent to sell well."

In spite of the company's legal problems, the 20th century ended on a high note for Microsoft. In March 1999, Internet Explorer 5.0 was introduced. Within one week, more than one million consumers had **downloaded** the new version. As the millennium drew to a close Microsoft had more than 30,000 employees and a **net income** of £4.9 billion ($7.79 billion).

"It's etched in our brains: Don't get complacent."

MICROSOFT EXECUTIVE JEFF RAIKES,
ON MICROSOFT'S WORK PHILOSOPHY

Microsoft has been accused of violating anti-trust laws – in the US and abroad – since the late 1990s

LIFE AT MICROSOFT

In some ways, the Microsoft workplace is more relaxed and informal than the environment one might find at other corporations. But the computer programmers, office administrators and other staff employed by Microsoft know that they are working for bosses who expect the best. Microsoft employees work hard and put in long hours, but they are rewarded with lavish holiday parties and company picnics (all-day fêtes for employees and their families). They're also rewarded with the knowledge that, thanks to stock options, the company they work for has more dollar millionaires on the payroll than any other corporation in the world. But Microsoft employees are aware of the fact that they are expected to follow certain rules. "If you're going to work for this company, you're going to rent a certain kind of hotel room and fly coach [economy] because that's business and anything else is luxury," explained Microsoft president and CEO Steve Ballmer.

Microsoft and the new millennium

Microsoft finally reached an agreement with the US Justice Department over the anti-trust lawsuit in 2001. According to the settlement terms Microsoft had to permit a panel of three independent monitors to work at the Microsoft "campus", with full access to the company's records and staff for five years.

The company also had to provide other software companies such as Netscape with information which allowed them to develop programs that interacted with Microsoft operating systems as easily as Microsoft's own products. Microsoft also agreed to donate money, in the form of software, computers and training, to more than 12,500 schools.

In the early years of the new millennium Microsoft entered a new dimension of the computer industry: video games. In the 1980s, electronic games had been designed to be downloaded and played on personal computers. Sony's PlayStation, introduced in 1995, was a console designed strictly for game-playing – its success and lucrative profits compelled Microsoft to jump into the business.

When Microsoft unveiled the high-powered Xbox gaming system in 2001 the console was an immediate hit with consumers. An online gaming experience called Xbox Live soon let gamers from all over the world link up and play multi-player

Microsoft agreed to make donations to schools as part of the 2001 anti-trust lawsuit settlement games and tournaments against one another. In 2005, Microsoft introduced the more powerful Xbox 360 system, which featured the most intense and graphically realistic games yet. "There has never been a more exciting time to be a gamer," Microsoft noted in a press release when Xbox 360 came out. "Xbox 360 will deliver mind-blowing experiences across multiple genres, no matter what your personal gaming preferences are." Microsoft's science-fiction combat game *Halo* and its sequels were especially popular and critically acclaimed games.

Microsoft continued fighting legal battles as the new millennium progressed. Most of the lawsuits brought against Microsoft were about the same thing: how Microsoft dominated the computer software market, often to the detriment of smaller companies. In many instances, Microsoft was able to settle the lawsuits out of court, thereby avoiding expensive trials and negative publicity. Yet Microsoft's common practice of donating software as part of its out-of-court settlements seemed to serve a double purpose to critics who pointed out that, in addition to bringing positive publicity to Microsoft, Microsoft also made sure that the schools receiving their software would not buy the competitors' software instead.

In June 2006, Microsoft announced that Bill Gates would be leaving his position as chief software architect, a title he had held since 2000, to devote more time to his work at the Bill and Melinda Gates Foundation, a philanthropic organisation created in 1999 by Gates and his wife Melinda (see page 29). Gates stated that he planned to continue as chairman and adviser of Microsoft. "I'm very lucky to have two passions that I feel are so important and so challenging. As I prepare for change I firmly believe the road ahead for Microsoft is as bright as ever," Gates said upon announcing his decision. Chief technical officer Ray Ozzie took over as Microsoft's chief software architect.

Microsoft's other founder, Paul Allen, had also stayed busy since leaving full-time duties at Microsoft in 1983, finding success with his investments in property and professional sports teams, and filling much of his time with philanthropic

By 2007, six years after launching the Xbox, Microsoft had become a heavyweight in the world of video gaming works. Through his charitable organisation, the Paul G. Allen Family Foundation, by 2003, he had donated more than £27 billion ($43 billion) to a variety of global causes, including education, the arts and scientific research.

As Gates prepared to leave the daily corporate world in 2006, Microsoft announced the release of a new version of Windows, called Vista. With a fresh design, easier organisation tools and the promise of a safer online experience, Microsoft believed Windows Vista would become the standard by which all operating systems would be measured. However, by 2009, Microsoft had improved its operating system yet again, launching Windows 7, which promised to simplify computing tasks and allow quicker access to programs. Windows 7 also included multi-touch technology, where areas on a touch-sensitive screen may be "tapped" using the fingers rather than clicked on using a mouse.

Microsoft made another big splash in the computer gaming industry in 2011 with the introduction of Kinect for Xbox 360, which turns the player's body into a game controller through movement and voice. "As breakthrough technologies like these reach scale, the resulting creativity and invention will open up a whole new world of possibilities for computing," said Craig Mundie, Microsoft's chief research and strategy officer.

The world of personal computers has evolved a great deal, and at break-neck speed, since 1975 when Paul Allen and Bill Gates founded Microsoft in Albuquerque, New Mexico. From the days of playing noughts and crosses on the Altair to the modern high-speed office applications of Windows 7, change has been the one constant in the world of computers. Through good times and bad, Microsoft has shown a rare ability to see those changes coming and, indeed, bring many of those changes about – an ability that has made it one of the true giants of the business world today.

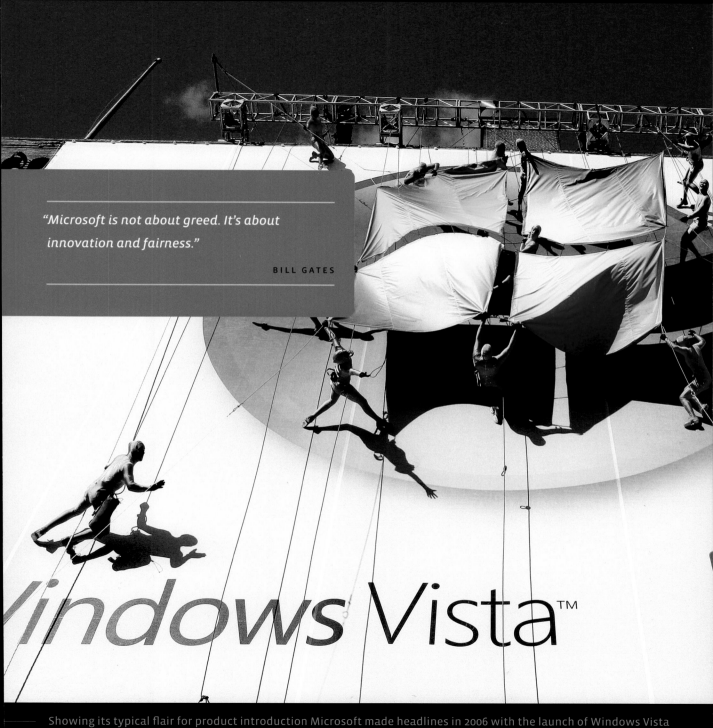

"Microsoft is not about greed. It's about innovation and fairness."

BILL GATES

Windows Vista™

Showing its typical flair for product introduction Microsoft made headlines in 2006 with the launch of Windows Vista

THE RICH LIFE

Bill Gates and Paul Allen are two of the wealthiest people in the world. While they both donate generously to a wide variety of charitable causes, they know how to enjoy the billions of dollars they've earned as well. Allen owns the Portland Trail Blazers professional basketball team (since 1988) and the Seattle Seahawks professional American football team (since 1997). He also owns a yacht that carries two helicopters and a submarine. Gates used a portion of his wealth to build a palatial house on Lake Washington in Medina, Washington, close to Microsoft's headquarters. The 3,716-square-metre house has a 30-car garage, a swimming pool with an underwater sound system, a cinema and a dining room that seats 150 guests. Gates also collects art and antiques. In 1994, he bought the Codex Leicester, a 72-page notebook that belonged to Renaissance artist Leonardo da Vinci, for £19.2 million ($30.8 million).

GLOSSARY

applications software that runs specific types of computer programs; examples include word processors and music-playing programs

anti-trust laws laws that protect companies from unfair business practices, such as one company gaining total control of a certain market

browser a program that allows a computer user to look through a collection of data, typically on the Internet; examples include Netscape and Internet Explorer

CD-ROM a computer disc that contains information that can be read but not changed; ROM stands for 'Read-Only Memory'

computer chip an electronic circuit that is a basic component of many electronic devices

cross-licencing the sharing of patents between two or more companies

default automatic action that is taken if other instructions are not given or received

downloaded copied, as data, to a computer (usually from an online, or Internet, source)

entrepreneurs people who start or organise a business of their own

genres distinctive types or categories

graphics displays generated by a computer on a screen or printer; graphics may include text, images or other visual displays

GUI (graphical user interface) a visual display on a screen that enables users to connect and interact with their computers

hardware the physical parts of a computer such as the central processing unit, discs, modem and leads

laptop computers small, lightweight computers that are designed to be portable and can be easily held on the user's lap

marketing advertising and promoting a product in order to increase sales

mouse a small device that controls the movement of an arrow, or pointer, on a computer screen; it assists in moving things on the screen or giving computer commands

monopoly exclusive control by one group over a commercial activity

net income the total income a company has after subtracting costs and expenses from total revenues

patent an official document that states who has the right to use, make or sell an invention

philanthropic describing a person or organisation who supports charitable causes through financial donations; the term also describes such efforts

prototype an original model that other, later copies are based upon

RAM (Random-Access Memory) memory chips that can be used by programs while a computer is in use

silicon a non-metallic chemical that is commonly used to make certain computer parts

software the programs that run a computer, or tell it how to operate

stock shared ownership in a company by many people who buy shares, or portions, of stock, hoping the company will make a profit and the stock value will increase

MICROSOFT MILESTONES

1967   Kent Evans and Bill Gates form the Lakeside
Programmers Club, later joined by Paul Allen and
Rick Welland.

1975   Gates and Allen found Micro-Soft. The hyphen is
later dropped.

1979   Microsoft moves to Bellvue, Washington.

1980   Steve Ballmer joins Microsoft. Microsoft
creates MS-DOS for IBM.

1983   Microsoft introduces Microsoft Word.

1985 Windows launched. Microsoft begins building new
corporate headquarters.

1986 Microsoft goes public.

1995 Windows 95 launched. MSN launched. Microsoft
Explorer launched.

1998 Massive lawsuit alleges Microsoft had broken
US anti-trust laws.

2001 Microsoft reaches agreement over anti-trust lawsuit.
Xbox online gaming system launched.

2006 Bill Gates steps down as chief software architect but
remains Microsoft chairman. He is succeeded by Ray Ozzie.

2009 Windows 7 launched.

2011 Kinect for Xbox 360 launched.

INDEX